Fire! Fire!

By Gail Gibbons

HarperCollins*Publishers*

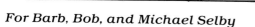

For Barb, Bob, and Michael Selby

FIRE! FIRE!
Copyright © 1984 by Gail Gibbons
Printed in Mexico. All rights reserved.

Library of Congress Cataloging-in-Publication Data
Gibbons, Gail.
  Fire! Fire!
  Summary: Explains how fire fighters fight fires
in the city, in the country, in the forest, and on the
waterfront.
  1. Fire prevention—Juvenile literature. 2. Fire
extinction—Juvenile literature. [1. Fire extinction.
2. Fire fighters] I. Title.
TH9148.G47 1984   628.9′25   83-46162
ISBN 0-690-04417-8.—ISBN 0-690-04416-X (lib. bdg.)
ISBN 0-06-446058-4 (pbk.)

Special thanks to

John Mulligan, Richard J. Sheirer, and
George A. Willett of the New York City
Fire Department;

Nick Nicholson, Gesualdo Schneider,
and Robert Shetsinger of the Montpelier
(Vermont) Fire Department;

Russell Barrett, Nelson Blackburn, and
Jay Lackey of the Vermont Department
of Forest and Parks;

William Field, volunteer firefighter of
the Chelsea (Vermont) Volunteer Fire
Department;

Carla Pembroke, Tom Pembroke, and
Phil Noyes, Sr., of the Middlesex Fire
Equipment Co., Montpelier, Vermont;

Maxim Motor Co., Inc. of Middleboro,
Massachusetts.

In an apartment house, a breeze has blown a towel up into the flame of a hot stove. A fire begins. The smoke alarm screams.

A phone call alerts the fire-dispatch center. Instantly,
a dispatcher calls the firehouse nearest the fire.

alarm room

12 WEST STREET...
12 WEST STREET...
12 WEST STREET...

A loudspeaker blares out the address of the fire, and the firefighters go into action. They slide down brass poles to the ground floor, where the fire engines are, and hurry into their fire-fighting gear.

Then they take their positions on their engines.

The big trucks roar out of the firehouse.
Sirens scream and lights flash.

The fire engines arrive at the scene.

The fire is bigger now.

The fire chief is in charge. He decides the best way
to fight this fire.

Hoses are pulled from the trucks.

Each separate fire truck is called a "company."

Each separate company has an officer in charge.

The fire chief tells each officer in charge what he wants the firefighters to do.

Firefighters are ordered to search the building to make sure no one is still inside.

A man is trapped. A ladder tower is swung into action. The man is rescued quickly.

At the same time, an aerial ladder is taking other firefighters to the floor above the fire.

Inside, the firefighters attach a hose to the building's standpipe. Water is sprayed onto the fire to keep it from moving up through the apartment house.

Now the aerial ladder is swung over to the roof of the burning building.

Firefighters break holes in the roof and windows to let out poisonous gases, heat, and smoke before they can cause a bad explosion. There's less danger now for the firefighters working inside the building.

Firefighters are battling the blaze from the outside of the building, too. Fire hoses carry water from the fire hydrants to the trucks.

pumper truck

pumper truck

pumper truck

discharge hose   soft-suction hoses

Pumps in the fire trucks control the water pressure and push the water up through the discharge hoses. Streams of water hit the burning building and buildings next door to keep the fire from spreading.

The fire is under control.

The fire is out.

The firefighters clean up the rubble.

Back at the firehouse, they clean their equipment
and make an official report on the fire.

City firefighters take turns living at their firehouse.

There are firefighters on duty day and night.

Between alarms, they practice and train.

They teach people fire prevention, too.

 **In the country...**

A barn has caught fire. A spark from an old electrical wire
has ignited some hay.

An emergency call is made to the fire-dispatch center.
This is a "central" fire-dispatch center for several country towns.

The dispatcher calls the volunteer firefighters in the town where the fire is. They get the message on their beepers.

Volunteer firefighters must leave their jobs or homes to answer a fire alarm, day or night. They don't live at the firehouse.

The volunteers hurry into their fire-fighting gear that they keep in their cars.

Some go to the firehouse to get the fire trucks.

Others will meet the trucks at the fire.

fire chief

chief's car

pumper truck

Here come the volunteers.

There isn't a fire hydrant here to supply water.

The pumper truck carries its own water. It pumps the water through the hose onto the fire.

tanker truck

portable water tank

The pumper truck runs out of water. A tanker truck is standing by to help out.

This fire is big! It might spread to the farmhouse.
The fire chief calls the dispatch center for more
equipment and firefighters. Another town is called for
help. This time an alarm is sounded from the firehouse.

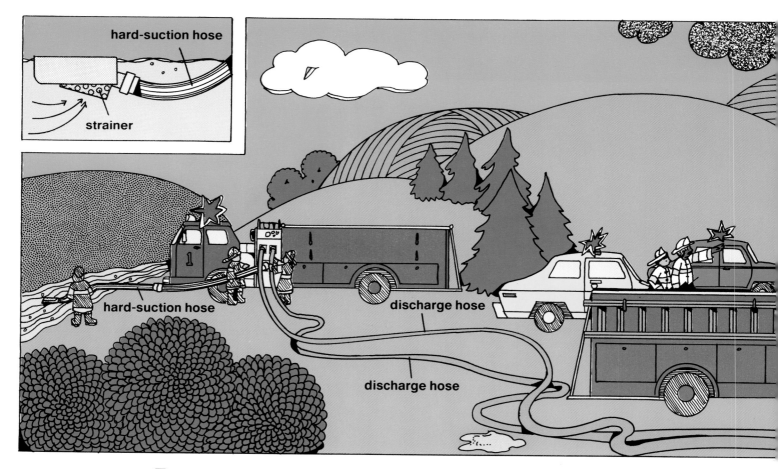

hard-suction hose

strainer

hard-suction hose

discharge hose

discharge hose

Two more pumper trucks arrive with volunteers.
There is a stream nearby. Water from the stream is
sucked through a hose into one pumper truck, then
pumped along to the other trucks.

The trucks spray water on the fire. The fire dies down.

The fire is out.

The farmhouse is saved.

The chief makes notes for his official report while
the firefighters help clean up.

The volunteers return to their firehouses to clean their trucks and equipment.

They will go back to their jobs and homes until they are called again.

 In the forest...

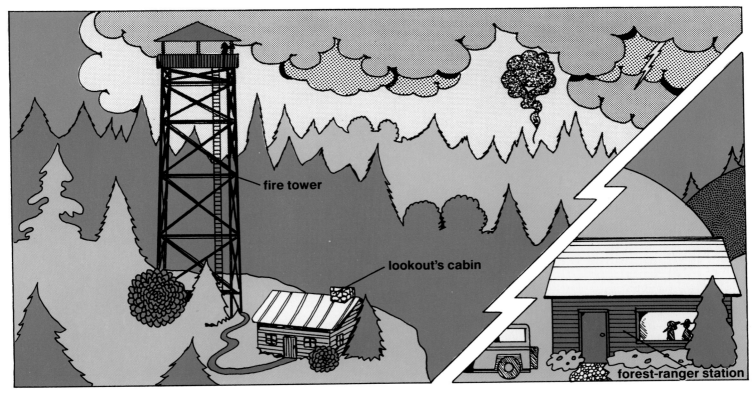

fire tower

lookout's cabin

forest-ranger station

Lightning has struck. It hasn't rained for a long time, and the ground and trees are dry. A fire begins.

In a fire tower, a lookout spots a plume of smoke. He radios the forest-ranger station to report the fire.

In moments, propeller planes fly in to help.
Smoke jumpers in their jumpsuits parachute down
to the scene. The fire-fighting supplies are dropped in.

The firefighters cut down trees and dig a fire stop—
a cleared area in front of the fire. A bulldozer arrives
to help clear, too. The ground is doused with water.
Now the fire can't spread.

Overhead, a plane sprays chemicals to smother
the flames.

The fire is over.

The smoke jumpers and supplies are picked up.

Back at the forest-ranger station, a fire-report form is filled out and filed.

Some time later, new young trees will be planted to help the damaged forest grow again.

 **On the waterfront...**

fireboat

fireboat

Some oily rags in an old pier building have begun to burn. The fire faces out over the water, and fire trucks can't get close enough to fight it. Fireboats—floating fire companies—must answer the alarm.

water nozzle

The fireboats aim their water nozzles at the pier
building. Big pumps in the boats suck up large amounts
of water and force it through the nozzles. Jets of water
stream onto the fire.

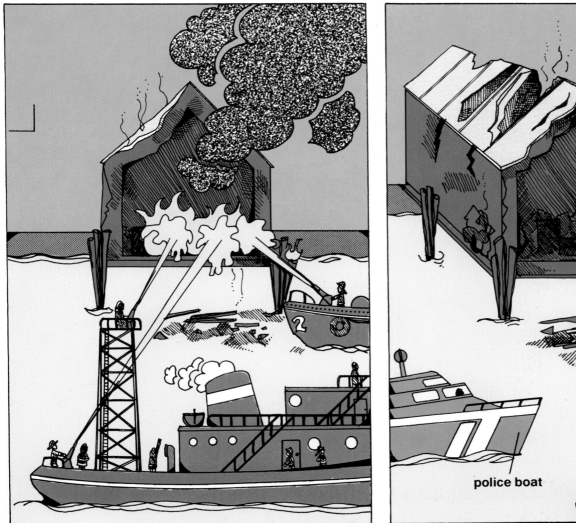

police boat

The fire sizzles and crackles. The fire is out.

The firefighters clean up and write their report.
Back with the other fireboats, they will patrol the
waters, on the alert for the next fire emergency.

Different kinds of fire!
Different kinds of firefighters!

They are ready to fight a fire the moment they are needed.

Other fire-fighting equipment

Fire extinguishers are used to put out small fires. They spray a chemical to smother the flames.

Flame-resistant suits are used in very hot fires to protect firefighters from the heat and flames.

Fire escapes are staircases permanently attached to the outsides of tall buildings. People can climb down them to safety.

Helicopters are called in to rescue people trapped in very high buildings.

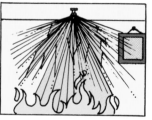

Sprinkler systems inside buildings automatically spray water if a fire begins.

Life nets or **air bags** can be placed under a window of a burning building so that people can jump to safety.

Foam-carrying trucks are needed to fight oil and gas fires. Water cannot be used on these fires, so the trucks spray a layer of foam on the flames to suffocate them.

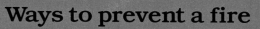

Ways to prevent a fire

Fires can be accidentally started by people of any age.

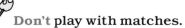 Don't play with matches.

 Don't leave anything burnable on or near a stove.

 Don't overload electrical outlets.
Don't use electrical cords that are old and frayed.

 Don't keep rags that are soaked with grease, oil, or paint.

 Don't smoke in bed.

 Don't start a barbecue fire with kerosene or gasoline.

 Don't leave rubbish or flammable liquids near a furnace, radiator, stove, or other heat source.

 Don't leave an iron while it is still hot.

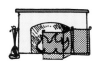 Don't use a wood stove or fireplace that has a dirty chimney.
Don't leave an unguarded fire.

 Don't leave a campfire until it is completely out.

 Make regular checks throughout your house for any fire hazards.

What to do if there is a fire...

1. Shout loud to warn other people in the building.

2. Get out of the building immediately.
   If the room is smoky, crawl on the floor.
   The air near the floor will be cooler and clearer.

3. If a door is hot, don't open it.
   There might be a fire behind it.
   Go to another exit.

4. Close the door behind you when you leave a room.
   It will help keep the fire from spreading.

5. Once you are outside the building, call the fire department from the nearest phone. If you don't know the fire department's phone number, dial the operator. (In some areas, there is a special emergency number, 911.) Give the complete address of the building—the number, street, city or town, and state.
   If there is a fire-alarm box nearby, use it.

6. Don't go back into the building for any reason.
   The firefighters will be there to help.

"Stop, drop, and roll"

If your clothes catch fire, stop—don't move.
Drop to your knees, then roll on the ground to smother the flames.

These rules are from a list approved by the Montpelier (Vermont) Fire Department.
Your local fire department will have a complete list of rules for your own area.

7601